Personal Inforı
This planner belor.

Address:

_____

Home & Mobile Number:

_____

Email address:

_____

	year at a glance	01 january	02 february	03 march	04 april	05 may	06 june
1							
2							
3							
4							
5							
6							
7							
8							
9							
10							
11							
12							
13							
14							
15							
16							
17							
18							
19							
20							
21							
22							
23							
24							
25							
26							
27							
28							
29							
30							
31							

year at a glance

	07 july	08 august	09 september	10 october	11 november	12 december
1						
2						
3						
4						
5						
6						
7						
8						
9						
10						
11						
12						
13						
14						
15						
16						
17						
18						
19						
20						
21						
22						
23						
24						
25						
26						
27						
28						
29						
30						
31						

FUCK ASSHOLE PISSFLAPS TWAT SHIT CUNT COCK TURD SHITHEAD WANKER BULLSHIT ASS DICKSPLAT JIZZ BOLLOCKS SPUNKBUBBLE MINGE

monthly summary

three things to look
forward to this month

1

2

3

birthdays

school holidays, inset
days or days off

one thing new I'll try
this month

Doodles for the
month

important things to remember this month

Fuck

Days of the fucking week

sunday	monday	tuesday	wednesday

thursday

friday

saturday

Jan Feb Mar
Apr May Jun
Jul Aug Sep
Oct Nov Dec

monthly goals

notes

monthly summary

three things to look forward to this month

1

2

3

birthdays

school holidays, inset days or days off

one thing new I'll try this month

important things to remember this month

Doodles for the month

Days of the fucking week

sunday	monday	tuesday	wednesday

thursday

friday

saturday

Jan Feb Mar
Apr May Jun
Jul Aug Sep
Oct Nov Dec

monthly goals

notes

monthly summary

three things to look
forward to this month

1

2

3

birthdays

school holidays, inset
days or days off

one thing new I'll try
this month

important things to remember this month

Doodles for the
month

Days of the fucking week

sunday	monday	tuesday	wednesday

thursday	friday	saturday

Jan Feb Mar
Apr May Jun
Jul Aug Sep
Oct Nov Dec

monthly goals

notes

monthly summary

three things to look forward to this month

1

2

3

birthdays

school holidays, inset days or days off

one thing new I'll try this month

important things to remember this month

Doodles for the month

Days of the fucking week

sunday	monday	tuesday	wednesday

thursday	friday	saturday

Jan Feb Mar
Apr May Jun
Jul Aug Sep
Oct Nov Dec

monthly goals

notes

monthly summary

three things to look
forward to this month

1

2

3

birthdays

school holidays, inset
days or days off

one thing new I'll try
this month

important things to remember this month

Doodles for the
month

Days of the fucking week

sunday	monday	tuesday	wednesday

thursday	friday	saturday

Jan Feb Mar
Apr May Jun
Jul Aug Sep
Oct Nov Dec

monthly goals

notes

monthly summary

three things to look forward to this month

1

2

3

birthdays

school holidays, inset days or days off

one thing new I'll try this month

important things to remember this month

Doodles for the month

Days of the fucking week

sunday	monday	tuesday	wednesday

thursday	friday	saturday

Jan Feb Mar
Apr May Jun
Jul Aug Sep
Oct Nov Dec

monthly goals

notes

Hey buddy...
fuck you.

monthly summary

three things to look
forward to this month

1

2

3

birthdays

school holidays, inset
days or days off

one thing new I'll try
this month

important things to remember this month

Doodles for the
month

Days of the fucking week

sunday	monday	tuesday	wednesday

thursday

friday

saturday

Jan Feb Mar
Apr May Jun
Jul Aug Sep
Oct Nov Dec

monthly goals

notes

monthly summary

three things to look
forward to this month

1

2

3

birthdays

school holidays, inset
days or days off

one thing new I'll try
this month

important things to remember this month

Doodles for the
month

Days of the fucking week

sunday	monday	tuesday	wednesday

thursday	friday	saturday

| Jan Feb Mar |
| Apr May Jun |
| Jul Aug Sep |
| Oct Nov Dec |

monthly goals

notes

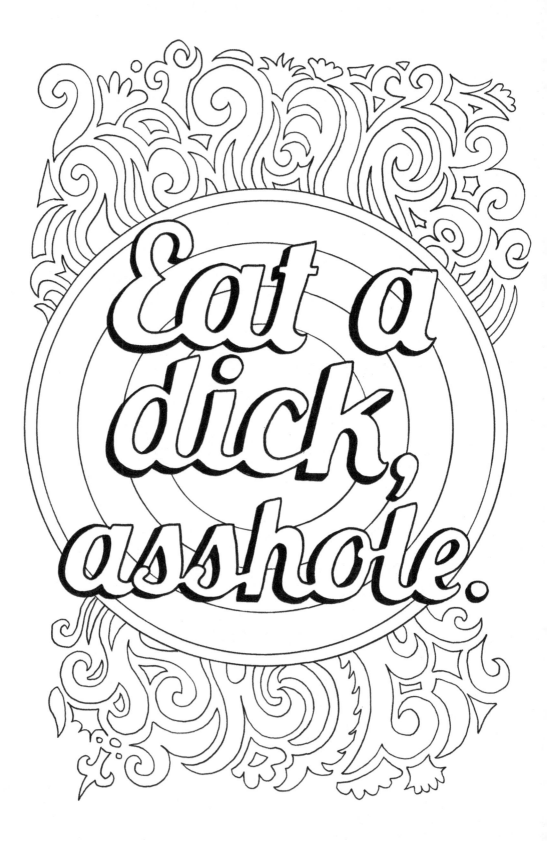

monthly summary

three things to look forward to this month

1

2

3

one thing new I'll try this month

Doodles for the month

birthdays

school holidays, inset days or days off

important things to remember this month

Days of the fucking week

sunday	monday	tuesday	wednesday

thursday	friday	saturday

monthly goals

notes

monthly summary

three things to look
forward to this month

1

2

3

birthdays

school holidays, inset
days or days off

one thing new I'll try
this month

important things to remember this month

Doodles for the
month

Days of the fucking week

sunday	monday	tuesday	wednesday

thursday	friday	saturday

Jan Feb Mar
Apr May Jun
Jul Aug Sep
Oct Nov Dec

monthly goals

notes

monthly summary

three things to look
forward to this month

1

2

3

birthdays

school holidays, inset
days or days off

one thing new I'll try
this month

important things to remember this month

Doodles for the
month

Days of the fucking week

sunday	monday	tuesday	wednesday

thursday	friday	saturday

Jan Feb Mar
Apr May Jun
Jul Aug Sep
Oct Nov Dec

monthly goals

notes

monthly summary

three things to look
forward to this month

1

2

3

birthdays

school holidays, inset
days or days off

one thing new I'll try
this month

important things to remember this month

Doodles for the
month

Days of the fucking week

sunday	monday	tuesday	wednesday

thursday

friday

saturday

Jan Feb Mar
Apr May Jun
Jul Aug Sep
Oct Nov Dec

monthly goals

notes

some fucking bullet journal dots or whatever

meal planner

sunday
_____

monday
_____

tuesday
_____

wednesday
_____

thursday
_____

friday
_____

saturday
_____

☐
sunday

☐
wednesday

☐
thursday

☐
monday

☐
tuesday

☐
friday

☐
saturday

☐ sunday

meal planner

sunday
_____

monday
_____

tuesday
_____

wednesday
_____

thursday
_____

friday
_____

saturday

☐ wednesday

☐ thursday

☐ monday

☐ tuesday

☐ friday

☐ saturday

meal planner

sunday
_____

monday
_____

tuesday
_____

wednesday
_____

thursday
_____

friday
_____

saturday

☐ sunday

☐ wednesday

☐ thursday

□ monday

□ tuesday

□ friday

□ saturday

☐ sunday

meal planner

sunday
_____

monday
_____

tuesday
_____

wednesday
_____

thursday
_____

friday
_____

saturday

☐ wednesday

☐ thursday

☐ monday

☐ tuesday

☐ friday

☐ saturday

meal planner

sunday
_____

monday
_____

tuesday
_____

wednesday
_____

thursday
_____

friday
_____

saturday

☐ sunday

☐ wednesday

☐ thursday

□ monday

□ tuesday

□ friday

□ saturday

□ sunday

meal planner

sunday
_____

monday
_____

tuesday
_____

wednesday
_____

thursday
_____

friday
_____

saturday

□ wednesday

□ thursday

☐ monday

☐ tuesday

☐ friday

☐ saturday

meal planner

sunday
_____

monday
_____

tuesday
_____

wednesday
_____

thursday
_____

friday
_____

saturday

☐ sunday

☐ wednesday

☐ thursday

□ monday

□ tuesday

□ friday

□ saturday

meal planner

sunday

---

monday

---

tuesday

---

wednesday

---

thursday

---

friday

---

saturday

☐
sunday

☐
wednesday

☐
thursday

☐ monday

☐ tuesday

☐ friday

☐ saturday

meal planner

sunday
_____

monday
_____

tuesday
_____

wednesday
_____

thursday
_____

friday
_____

saturday

☐ sunday

☐ wednesday

☐ thursday

☐ monday

☐ tuesday

☐ friday

☐ saturday

meal planner

sunday
_____

monday
_____

tuesday
_____

wednesday
_____

thursday
_____

friday
_____

saturday

sunday

wednesday

thursday

□
monday

□
tuesday

□
friday

□
saturday

☐ sunday

meal planner

sunday
_____

monday
_____

tuesday
_____

wednesday
_____

thursday
_____

friday
_____

saturday

☐ wednesday

☐ thursday

monday

tuesday

friday

saturday

meal planner

sunday
_____

monday
_____

tuesday
_____

wednesday
_____

thursday
_____

friday
_____

saturday

☐
wednesday

☐
thursday

☐ monday

☐ tuesday

☐ friday

☐ saturday

meal planner

sunday

monday

tuesday

wednesday

thursday

friday

saturday

☐ sunday

☐ wednesday

☐ thursday

☐ monday

☐ tuesday

☐ friday

☐ saturday

meal planner

sunday
_____

monday
_____

tuesday
_____

wednesday
_____

thursday
_____

friday
_____

saturday

☐ sunday

☐ wednesday

☐ thursday

☐ monday

☐ tuesday

☐ friday

☐ saturday

meal planner

sunday

_____

monday

_____

tuesday

_____

wednesday

_____

thursday

_____

friday

_____

saturday

_____

☐ sunday

☐ wednesday

☐ thursday

☐ monday

☐ tuesday

☐ friday

☐ saturday

☐ sunday

meal planner

sunday
—————————————————————
monday
—————————————————————
tuesday
—————————————————————
wednesday
—————————————————————
thursday
—————————————————————
friday
—————————————————————
saturday

☐ wednesday

☐ thursday

□ monday

□ tuesday

□ friday

□ saturday

meal planner

sunday
_____

monday
_____

tuesday
_____

wednesday
_____

thursday
_____

friday
_____

saturday

☐ sunday

☐ wednesday

☐ thursday

monday

tuesday

friday

saturday

meal planner

sunday

monday

tuesday

wednesday

thursday

friday

saturday

☐ sunday

☐ wednesday

☐ thursday

☐ monday

☐ tuesday

☐ friday

☐ saturday

meal planner

sunday
_____

monday
_____

tuesday
_____

wednesday
_____

thursday
_____

friday
_____

saturday

☐ sunday

☐ wednesday

☐ thursday

☐ monday

☐ tuesday

☐ friday

☐ saturday

meal planner

sunday
_____

monday
_____

tuesday
_____

wednesday
_____

thursday
_____

friday
_____

saturday

☐ sunday

☐ wednesday

☐ thursday

☐ monday

☐ tuesday

☐ friday

☐ saturday

□ sunday

meal planner

sunday
_____

monday
_____

tuesday
_____

wednesday
_____

thursday
_____

friday
_____

saturday

□ wednesday

□ thursday

□ monday

□ tuesday

□ friday

□ saturday

meal planner

sunday
---

monday
---

tuesday
---

wednesday
---

thursday
---

friday
---

saturday

wednesday

thursday

☐
monday

☐
tuesday

☐
friday

☐
saturday

meal planner

sunday
_____

monday
_____

tuesday
_____

wednesday
_____

thursday
_____

friday
_____

saturday

☐
sunday

☐
wednesday

☐
thursday

☐ monday

☐ tuesday

☐ friday

☐ saturday

☐ sunday

meal planner

sunday
―――――――――――――――――
monday
―――――――――――――――――
tuesday
―――――――――――――――――
wednesday
―――――――――――――――――
thursday
―――――――――――――――――
friday
―――――――――――――――――
saturday

☐ wednesday

☐ thursday

□
monday

□
tuesday

□
friday

□
saturday

meal planner

sunday
_____

monday
_____

tuesday
_____

wednesday
_____

thursday
_____

friday
_____

saturday

☐ sunday

☐ wednesday

☐ thursday

☐ monday

☐ tuesday

☐ friday

☐ saturday

meal planner

sunday
_____

monday
_____

tuesday
_____

wednesday
_____

thursday
_____

friday
_____

saturday

☐ sunday

☐ wednesday

☐ thursday

☐ monday

☐ tuesday

☐ friday

☐ saturday

meal planner

sunday
_____

monday
_____

tuesday
_____

wednesday
_____

thursday
_____

friday
_____

saturday

☐ sunday

☐ wednesday

☐ thursday

☐ monday

☐ tuesday

☐ friday

☐ saturday

meal planner

sunday
_____

monday
_____

tuesday
_____

wednesday
_____

thursday
_____

friday
_____

saturday

☐ sunday

☐ wednesday

☐ thursday

☐ monday

☐ tuesday

☐ friday

☐ saturday

meal planner

sunday
_____

monday
_____

tuesday
_____

wednesday
_____

thursday
_____

friday
_____

saturday

☐ sunday

☐ wednesday

☐ thursday

☐ monday

☐ tuesday

☐ friday

☐ saturday

□ sunday

meal planner

sunday
———————————————————————
monday
———————————————————————
tuesday
———————————————————————
wednesday
———————————————————————
thursday
———————————————————————
friday
———————————————————————
saturday

□ wednesday

□ thursday

☐ monday

☐ tuesday

☐ friday

☐ saturday

☐ sunday

meal planner

sunday
_____

monday
_____

tuesday
_____

wednesday
_____

thursday
_____

friday
_____

saturday

☐ wednesday

☐ thursday

monday

tuesday

friday

saturday

☐ sunday

meal planner

sunday
_____

monday
_____

tuesday
_____

wednesday
_____

thursday
_____

friday
_____

saturday

☐ wednesday

☐ thursday

☐ monday

☐ tuesday

☐ friday

☐ saturday

meal planner

sunday

_____

monday

_____

tuesday

_____

wednesday

_____

thursday

_____

friday

_____

saturday

☐ sunday

☐ wednesday

☐ thursday

☐ monday

☐ tuesday

☐ friday

☐ saturday

meal planner

sunday

monday

tuesday

wednesday

thursday

friday

saturday

☐
sunday

☐
wednesday

☐
thursday

☐ monday

☐ tuesday

☐ friday

☐ saturday

meal planner

sunday
_____

monday
_____

tuesday
_____

wednesday
_____

thursday
_____

friday
_____

saturday

☐ sunday

☐ wednesday

☐ thursday

□
monday

□
tuesday

□
friday

□
saturday

☐ sunday

meal planner

sunday
———————————————————
monday
———————————————————
tuesday
———————————————————
wednesday
———————————————————
thursday
———————————————————
friday
———————————————————
saturday

☐ wednesday

☐ thursday

☐ monday

☐ tuesday

☐ friday

☐ saturday

□ sunday

meal planner

sunday
_____

monday
_____

tuesday
_____

wednesday
_____

thursday
_____

friday
_____

saturday

□ wednesday

□ thursday

□ monday

□ tuesday

□ friday

□ saturday

meal planner

sunday
_____

monday
_____

tuesday
_____

wednesday
_____

thursday
_____

friday
_____

saturday

☐ sunday

☐ wednesday

☐ thursday

☐ monday

☐ tuesday

☐ friday

☐ saturday

meal planner

sunday
_____

monday
_____

tuesday
_____

wednesday
_____

thursday
_____

friday
_____

saturday

☐ sunday

☐ wednesday

☐ thursday

☐
monday

☐
tuesday

☐
friday

☐
saturday

meal planner

sunday
_____

monday
_____

tuesday
_____

wednesday
_____

thursday
_____

friday
_____

saturday

☐ sunday

☐ wednesday

☐ thursday

☐ monday

☐ tuesday

☐ friday

☐ saturday

meal planner

sunday
———————————————
monday
———————————————
tuesday
———————————————
wednesday
———————————————
thursday
———————————————
friday
———————————————
saturday

☐ sunday

☐ wednesday

☐ thursday

□ monday

□ tuesday

□ friday

□ saturday

meal planner

sunday
_____

monday
_____

tuesday
_____

wednesday
_____

thursday
_____

friday
_____

saturday

☐
sunday

☐
wednesday

☐
thursday

☐
monday

☐
tuesday

☐
friday

☐
saturday

meal planner

sunday
_____

monday
_____

tuesday
_____

wednesday
_____

thursday
_____

friday
_____

saturday

☐ sunday

☐ wednesday

☐ thursday

☐ monday

☐ tuesday

☐ friday

☐ saturday

meal planner

sunday
_____

monday
_____

tuesday
_____

wednesday
_____

thursday
_____

friday
_____

saturday

□ wednesday

□ thursday

☐ monday

☐ tuesday

☐ friday

☐ saturday

meal planner

sunday
_____

monday
_____

tuesday
_____

wednesday
_____

thursday
_____

friday
_____

saturday

☐ sunday

☐ wednesday

☐ thursday

☐ monday

☐ tuesday

☐ friday

☐ saturday

☐ sunday

meal planner

sunday
_____

monday
_____

tuesday
_____

wednesday
_____

thursday
_____

friday
_____

saturday

☐ wednesday

☐ thursday

☐
monday

☐
tuesday

☐
friday

☐
saturday

meal planner

sunday
―――――――――――――――――――――――

monday
―――――――――――――――――――――――

tuesday
―――――――――――――――――――――――

wednesday
―――――――――――――――――――――――

thursday
―――――――――――――――――――――――

friday
―――――――――――――――――――――――

saturday

☐
sunday

☐
wednesday

☐
thursday

☐
monday

☐
tuesday

☐
friday

☐
saturday

meal planner

sunday
_____

monday
_____

tuesday
_____

wednesday
_____

thursday
_____

friday
_____

saturday

☐ sunday

☐ wednesday

☐ thursday

□ monday

□ tuesday

□ friday

□ saturday

meal planner

sunday
_____
monday
_____
tuesday
_____
wednesday
_____
thursday
_____
friday
_____
saturday

☐ sunday

☐ wednesday

☐ thursday

monday

tuesday

friday

saturday

meal planner

sunday
_____

monday
_____

tuesday
_____

wednesday
_____

thursday
_____

friday
_____

saturday

☐ sunday

☐ wednesday

☐ thursday

monday

tuesday

friday

saturday

meal planner

sunday
_____

monday
_____

tuesday
_____

wednesday
_____

thursday
_____

friday
_____

saturday

sunday

wednesday

thursday

☐ monday

☐ tuesday

☐ friday

☐ saturday

meal planner

sunday
_____
monday
_____
tuesday
_____
wednesday
_____
thursday
_____
friday
_____
saturday

☐
sunday

☐
wednesday

☐
thursday

monday

tuesday

friday

saturday

meal planner

sunday
_____

monday
_____

tuesday
_____

wednesday
_____

thursday
_____

friday
_____

saturday

☐
sunday

☐
wednesday

☐
thursday

☐ monday

☐ tuesday

☐ friday

☐ saturday

meal planner

sunday
---
monday
---
tuesday
---
wednesday
---
thursday
---
friday
---
saturday

☐ sunday

☐ wednesday

☐ thursday

☐ monday

☐ tuesday

☐ friday

☐ saturday

meal planner

sunday
_____
monday
_____
tuesday
_____
wednesday
_____
thursday
_____
friday
_____
saturday

☐ sunday

☐ wednesday

☐ thursday

☐ monday

☐ tuesday

☐ friday

☐ saturday

monthly habit tracker

1																								
2																								
3																								
4																								
5																								
6																								
7																								
8																								
9																								
10																								
11																								
12																								
13																								
14																								
15																								
16																								
17																								
18																								
19																								
20																								
21																								
22																								
23																								
24																								
25																								
26																								
27																								
28																								
29																								
30																								
31																								

1																					
2																					
3																					
4																					
5																					
6																					
7																					
8																					
9																					
10																					
11																					
12																					
13																					
14																					
15																					
16																					
17																					
18																					
19																					
20																					
21																					
22																					
23																					
24																					
25																					
26																					
27																					
28																					
29																					
30																					
31																					

monthly habit tracker

	1																											
	2																											
	3																											
	4																											
	5																											
	6																											
	7																											
	8																											
	9																											
	10																											
	11																											
	12																											
	13																											
	14																											
	15																											
	16																											
	17																											
	18																											
	19																											
	20																											
	21																											
	22																											
	23																											
	24																											
	25																											
	26																											
	27																											
	28																											
	29																											
	30																											
	31																											

1																									
2																									
3																									
4																									
5																									
6																									
7																									
8																									
9																									
10																									
11																									
12																									
13																									
14																									
15																									
16																									
17																									
18																									
19																									
20																									
21																									
22																									
23																									
24																									
25																									
26																									
27																									
28																									
29																									
30																									
31																									

monthly habit tracker

	1																			
	2																			
	3																			
	4																			
	5																			
	6																			
	7																			
	8																			
	9																			
	10																			
	11																			
	12																			
	13																			
	14																			
	15																			
	16																			
	17																			
	18																			
	19																			
	20																			
	21																			
	22																			
	23																			
	24																			
	25																			
	26																			
	27																			
	28																			
	29																			
	30																			
	31																			

1																					
2																					
3																					
4																					
5																					
6																					
7																					
8																					
9																					
10																					
11																					
12																					
13																					
14																					
15																					
16																					
17																					
18																					
19																					
20																					
21																					
22																					
23																					
24																					
25																					
26																					
27																					
28																					
29																					
30																					
31																					

monthly habit tracker

	1
	2
	3
	4
	5
	6
	7
	8
	9
	10
	11
	12
	13
	14
	15
	16
	17
	18
	19
	20
	21
	22
	23
	24
	25
	26
	27
	28
	29
	30
	31

monthly habit tracker

1																				
2																				
3																				
4																				
5																				
6																				
7																				
8																				
9																				
10																				
11																				
12																				
13																				
14																				
15																				
16																				
17																				
18																				
19																				
20																				
21																				
22																				
23																				
24																				
25																				
26																				
27																				
28																				
29																				
30																				
31																				

monthly habit tracker

	1																					
	2																					
	3																					
	4																					
	5																					
	6																					
	7																					
	8																					
	9																					
	10																					
	11																					
	12																					
	13																					
	14																					
	15																					
	16																					
	17																					
	18																					
	19																					
	20																					
	21																					
	22																					
	23																					
	24																					
	25																					
	26																					
	27																					
	28																					
	29																					
	30																					
	31																					

monthly habit tracker

1																					
2																					
3																					
4																					
5																					
6																					
7																					
8																					
9																					
10																					
11																					
12																					
13																					
14																					
15																					
16																					
17																					
18																					
19																					
20																					
21																					
22																					
23																					
24																					
25																					
26																					
27																					
28																					
29																					
30																					
31																					

monthly habit tracker

1																				
2																				
3																				
4																				
5																				
6																				
7																				
8																				
9																				
10																				
11																				
12																				
13																				
14																				
15																				
16																				
17																				
18																				
19																				
20																				
21																				
22																				
23																				
24																				
25																				
26																				
27																				
28																				
29																				
30																				
31																				

1																								
2																								
3																								
4																								
5																								
6																								
7																								
8																								
9																								
10																								
11																								
12																								
13																								
14																								
15																								
16																								
17																								
18																								
19																								
20																								
21																								
22																								
23																								
24																								
25																								
26																								
27																								
28																								
29																								
30																								
31																								

put some fucking doodles here

put some fucking doodles here

put some fucking doodles here

put some fucking doodles here

put some fucking doodles here

put some fucking doodles here

put some fucking doodles here

put some fucking doodles here

put some fucking doodles here

put some fucking doodles here

contacts

name:
phone:
address:

email:

name:
phone:
address:

email:

name:
phone:
address:

email:

name:
phone:
address:

email:

name:
phone:
address:

email:

name:
phone:
address:

email:

name:
phone:
address:

email:

name:
phone:
address:

email:

name:
phone:
address:

email:

name:
phone:
address:

email:

contacts

name:

phone:

address:

email:

name:

phone:

address:

email:

name:

phone:

address:

email:

name:

phone:

address:

email:

name:

phone:

address:

email: ·

name:

phone:

address:

email:

name:

phone:

address:

email:

name:

phone:

address:

email:

name:

phone:

address:

email:

name:

phone:

address:

email:

contacts

name:

phone:

address:

email:

name:

phone:

address:

email:

name:

phone:

address:

email:

name:

phone:

address:

email:

name:

phone:

address:

email:

name:

phone:

address:

email:

name:

phone:

address:

email:

name:

phone:

address:

email:

name:

phone:

address:

email:

name:

phone:

address:

email:

name:

phone:

address:

email:

name:

phone:

address:

email:

name:

phone:

address:

email:

name:

phone:

address:

email:

name:

phone:

address:

email:

name:

phone:

address:

email:

name:

phone:

address:

email:

name:

phone:

address:

email:

name:

phone:

address:

email:

name:

phone:

address:

email:

contacts

name:

phone:

address:

email:

name:

phone:

address:

email:

name:

phone:

address:

email:

name:

phone:

address:

email:

name:

phone:

address:

email:

name:

phone:

address:

email:

name:

phone:

address:

email:

name:

phone:

address:

email:

name:

phone:

address:

email:

name:

phone:

address:

email:

notes

notes

notes

notes

notes

notes

notes

notes

notes

notes

notes

Made in the USA
Las Vegas, NV
08 July 2021